# People of the Bible

*The Bible through stories and pictures*

# Miracles
by the Sea

Art Director: Treld Bicknell

First published in the United States of America 1983
by Raintree Publishers, Inc.
205 West Highland Avenue, Milwaukee, Wisconsin 53203
in association with Belitha Press Ltd, London.

Conceived, designed and produced by Belitha Press Ltd,
40 Belitha Villas, London N1 1PD

Moody Press Edition 1984

ISBN 0-8024-0397-2

First published in Australia in paperback 1983
by Princeton Books Pty Ltd, PO Box 24, Cheltenham, Victoria 3192
in association with Raintree Childrens Books
205 West Highland Avenue, Milwaukee, Wisconsin 53203

ISBN 0-909091-22-6 (Australian)

Printed in Hong Kong by South China Printing Co.

Moody Press, a ministry of the Moody Bible Institute,
is designed for education, evangelization, and
edification. If we may assist you in knowing more
about Christ and the Christian life, please write us
without obligation: Moody Press, c/o MLM, Chicago,
Illinois 60610

# Miracles by the Sea

Retold by Ella K. Lindvall

Pictures by Chris Molan

MOODY PRESS
CHICAGO

One day Jesus, God's Son, was preaching on the shore. Many people came to hear Him. He saw two boats on the water nearby. One of them belonged to Simon. Jesus got into it and

asked Simon to push out a little into the lake.
Then He sat down and talked to the people
from the boat.

When He had finished teaching, Jesus said to Simon, "Now take the boat out into the deep water and let down the net so that you can catch some fish."

"I'll do what you tell me," said Simon. "But we've been fishing all night, and we haven't caught a single one."

Simon went out with his boat into the middle of the lake and let down the net. So many fish swam into it that it broke when Simon tried to pull it in. There were enough fish to fill two boats.

For nothing is too hard for God's Son to do.

Another day, Jesus and His friends sailed
across the lake. A great crowd of people was
waiting for Him on the other side.

Jesus talked to them about God's kingdom.
He saw that some of the people were sick, and
He made them well.

Late in the day, Jesus' disciples said to Him, "Send all these people away now. It is late, and they should go and buy food."

Jesus said, "You give them something to eat."

Andrew said, "There's a boy here who has five little loaves of bread and two fish. But that's not nearly enough to feed all these people."

Jesus said, "Bring the bread and fish to Me. And tell the people to rest on the grass."

Jesus thanked God for the food. Then He
broke the bread and fish. He gave the pieces to
His disciples. They began to hand them out to
the people. The men and women and children

ate as much as they wanted. Even so, there was enough left over to fill twelve baskets.

For nothing is too hard for God's Son to do.

Afterward Jesus sent the people home. Then He told the disciples to get into the boat. He walked up the hill to be alone with God, His Father.

It was dark now. Jesus' disciples began to sail toward the other side of the lake. Suddenly a great wind started to blow, and the sea became rough. Huge, frightening waves rolled the boat back and forth.

The disciples were a long way from land and in great danger. All at once they saw someone walking toward them on top of the stormy water. Now they were even more afraid. They were sure it was a ghost.

"Don't be frightened," Jesus called to them.
"It's I."

"If it's really You, Master," Peter said, "tell
me to come to you on the water."

"Come!" Jesus answered.

Peter got out of the boat. He started walking on top of the water toward Jesus. But the wind blew hard. The waves splashed. Peter became afraid, and he began to sink.

"Lord, save me!" he cried.

At once Jesus put out His hand and caught Peter. "Why didn't you keep on trusting Me?" Jesus asked.

Jesus and Peter got back into the boat. Right away the wind stopped blowing, and they were all safe.

The disciples had learned something. They said to Jesus, "You certainly are God's Son."

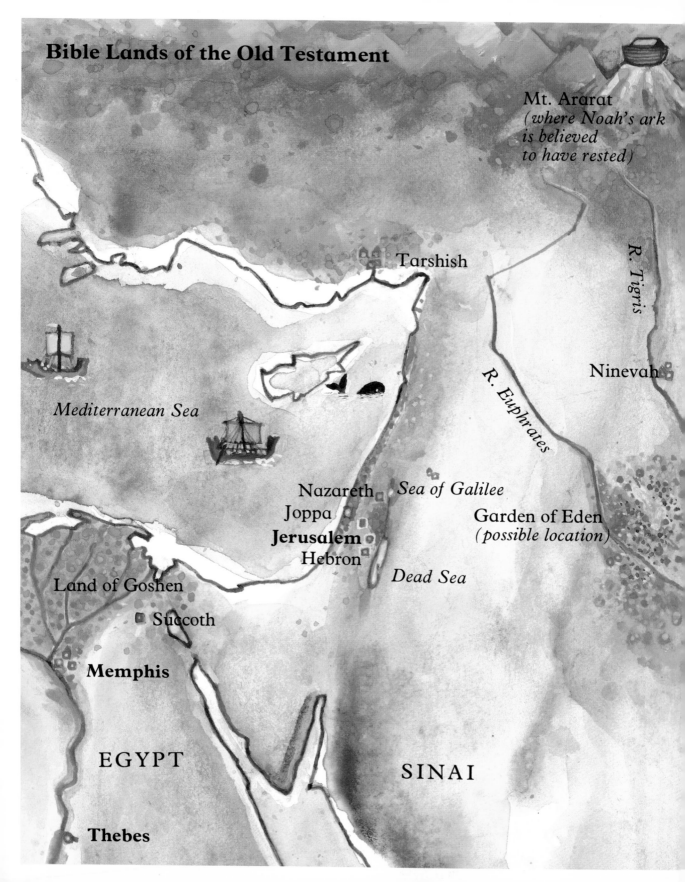

# Bible Lands of the Old Testament

Mt. Ararat
*(where Noah's ark
is believed
to have rested)*

Tarshish

*R. Tigris*

Ninevah

*R. Euphrates*

*Mediterranean Sea*

Nazareth    *Sea of Galilee*

Joppa

**Jerusalem**        Garden of Eden
                     *(possible location)*

Hebron

*Dead Sea*

Land of Goshen

Succoth

**Memphis**

EGYPT            SINAI

**Thebes**